SAWDUST TRAIL
PREACHER

Sawdust Trail Preacher

The Story of Billy Sunday

Betty Steele Everett

CLC ✦ PUBLICATIONS
Fort Washington, Pennsylvania 19034

Published by CLC ⋄ Publications

U.S.A.
P.O. Box 1449, Fort Washington, PA 19034

GREAT BRITAIN
51 The Dean, Alresford, Hants. SO24 9BJ

AUSTRALIA
P.O. Box 419M, Manunda, QLD 4879

NEW ZEALAND
10 MacArthur Street, Feilding

ISBN 0-87508-499-0

Printed in the United States of America

CONTENTS

1

WILLIE THE ORPHAN

YOUNG Willie Sunday listened as his older brother Edward explained why he was leaving the orphanage.

"You know you and I can only stay here until we're sixteen, Willie. And now I'm sixteen," Edward said. "I have to leave."

"Then I'm coming with you! I never wanted to come here! I won't stay without you! They can't make me!" Willie said, his temper rising.

Willie and Edward had been "orphans" for almost two years—since 1874 when their stepfather, Mr. Heizer, had suddenly just disappeared, leaving their mother with five children she could not take care of. Willie remembered how he had had to say goodbye to his dog Watch when they left the farm, and he could not forget how his mother had cried and prayed as they waited in Ames for the train that would take her sons away from her to the Soldiers' Orphan Home in Glenwood, Iowa.

"You won't be sixteen for two years yet, Willie—not until November 19, 1878," Edward pointed out. "You can stay here until then."

"I'm going with you!" Willie insisted. "I suppose you'll go back to Grandpa Corey's farm at Ames, won't you?''

Edward nodded. "It's where Mother is, and Leroy too—even if he is only a half-brother. He's the only one Mother's had with her, what with you and me here and Albert off in that home for the feeble-minded since the horse kicked him in the head. Poor little Libbie...what a shame she burned to death when her dress caught fire from that bonfire she was watching over."

Willie remembered his mother's father and the farm. Martin Corey had been one of Iowa's first settlers, and was called "Squire" by his neighbors. He had given the land for the Iowa Agricultural College at Ames when it was founded in 1858. On the rest of his land he had built a sawmill, a grainmill, and a sugar-cane mill.

"Squire" Corey wore a coonskin cap, rawhide boots, and blue jeans. He was a second cousin to Ulysses S. Grant, but when he was invited to the White House he turned down the invitation because of the expense of the trip, and the fact that he had no suit good enough to wear.

Willie Sunday had been sent to live on the farm with his Corey grandparents when he and his stepfather did not get along. He had lived there until 1874, when his mother had to leave the two-room log cabin where Willie had been born and move with her children into her parents' house. To cut expenses, Willie and Edward had then been sent to the Soldiers' Orphan Home.

Both "Squire" Corey and Willie had tempers

that flared easily, and they had had many stormy scenes. Yet Willie respected his grandfather, but it was his grandmother whom he loved and adored. When she died, he would not leave the casket unless absolutely necessary, and two days after the funeral he had worried his family by disappearing. His dog led them finally to Willie, lying across his grandmother's grave and sobbing. It was a cold winter's night, but Willie had spent most of it there on the ground.

Edward and Willie had qualified for the Soldiers' Orphan Home because their father had died while serving with the Twenty-third Iowa Infantry. Willie's father's family had come from Germany, where their name had been Sonntag, to live in Chambersburg, Pennsylvania. Willie's father had been a bricklayer, and then a farmer in Iowa. He had walked thirty miles from Ames to Des Moines to enlist in the Union Army in 1862.

Mr. Sunday did not live to see the end of the Civil War. After his regiment forded a partly frozen river, he and several others caught pneumonia. He died without ever seeing Willie, and was buried at Camp Patterson, Missouri.

One of the last letters Mrs. Sunday got from the battlefield told her that if the baby on the way was a boy, to name him William Ashley. No one knows where Willie's father got the name or why he wanted his newest son to have it, but Willie's mother followed her husband's instructions. With Willie, she had three sons to care for when her husband died: Albert, four; Edward, two; and little Willie.

With her government pension and help from her parents, Mrs. Sunday managed on the small farm for six years. Then she married Mr. Heizer and had two more children: Leroy and Libbie.

"You'll have to work hard on the farm," Edward warned Willie now.

"I know." It was not the hard work that worried Willie. He had milked cows morning and night, plowed, reaped, and made sorghum molasses in the sugar mill. What bothered Willie was whether he and his grandfather would be able to get along together any better now than they had two years before. He wanted to go with Edward, though, and so he did.

When the boys left the Orphan Home, Willie may have looked back and thought about the time he had lived there. It had not been a bad time. The discipline was strict but not too hard. Things had to be kept in place, and Willie learned habits of neatness and cleanliness that would stay with him all his life. He had even gotten an elementary school education at the Home, although all attempts at religious and Bible training had rolled off him. Willie's real reputation at the Home came from being the fastest runner and a good fighter.

The boys were welcomed back to the Corey home in Ames. The extra hands were welcome, and they were soon busy helping their grandfather and Roy to run the various businesses.

The work was still hard, and Willie and the "Squire" still got angry easily. The situation exploded one day when Willie's grandfather cursed him for something the teenager thought was not important.

"I'm leaving!" Willie announced.

He went to a friend's house, borrowed a horse, and rode eight miles to the county seat, the little town of Nevada. There Willie got a job as a hotel errand boy.

Willie was firm in his promise to himself never to go back home to live, but in a few months he decided to go back to see his mother. He stayed away from his job for two days, and when he got back to Nevada found he had been fired from his hotel job.

"You were gone longer than twenty-four hours!" the proprietor told him. "That should have been enough vacation for you!"

Getting fired may have seemed like a tragedy to Willie then, but it was really a blessing. He needed a job, and his new one was as stable boy for Colonel John Scott, a former lieutenant-governor of the state. The Colonel and his wife liked Willie and let him live in their house. They cared about his education, too, and helped him to go to high school in Nevada.

Willie earned $8 a month plus his room and board at the Scotts' and he got a job as janitor at the school to pay for his books and other needs.

The days were long for Willie and the work was

hard. He got up at 2 a.m., carried coal for the fourteen stoves at the school, kept all fourteen fires going all day, and swept and polished the floors. This was his janitor's job; the work for the Scotts came later, and so did his studying. But he got through high school.

Willie did not study all the time, though. In the summer he got to be known around the area as a good athlete and a very speedy runner. He won several Fourth of July races.

Willie was also getting a reputation for liking the girls and being willing to fight "at the drop of a hat," as the mayor once said about him.

One group who especially noticed Willie's speed and athletic ability was the Marshalltown fire brigade. This volunteer group needed a man like Willie to help them win in the fire fighting tournaments held with other brigades.

When they asked Willie to join them for the big annual tournament, he protested. "That's the day I graduate from high school."

The honor of being part of a fire brigade was so tempting that Willy joined anyway, and never did "graduate" from high school although he earned his diploma.

After he moved to Marshalltown, Billy Sunday (the name "Willie" must have seemed too juvenile now) found that fire fighting did not take all his time. He got a job with an undertaker for $3 a week. In those days undertakers often owned furniture stores too, and Billy worked there most of the time. Even with his job and belonging to the fire brigade, Billy found time to play on the Marshalltown baseball team.

Billy played in the outfield where his great speed turned what looked like hits into merely long outs. In 1883 Marshalltown won the Iowa state championship, and one of the men who noticed Billy was A.C. Anson, often called "Pop" or "Cap." He was the manager for the Chicago Whitestockings, a professional baseball team owned by A.G. Spalding.

"You can play ball with us," Anson told Billy. "And we can pay you a lot more than that undertaker. We'll pay you $60 a month!"

Billy could hardly believe it. Who wouldn't want to play professional baseball—especially with a team like the Chicago Whitestockings! They had won three pennants in a row from 1880 to 1882, wore expensive uniforms, stayed at the best hotels, and rode to the ballpark in a fancy open carriage pulled by white horses.

It was like a dream come true to the twenty-one-year-old Billy, and he did not need to hear any more from Mr. Anson.

"I'm going to Chicago and play baseball!" Billy told his employer, his team, and the fire brigade. "I'm going to play professional baseball!"

2

IN PROFESSIONAL BASEBALL

BILLY arrived in Chicago in 1883, wearing a sage-green suit that had cost him $6 and with $1 in his pocket. He was ready to play ball, but he did not make a big impression on his teammates.

The older, more experienced players looked Billy over carefully. "Hayseed!" they jeered. "Hick! Rube!"

Billy knew the only way to shut them up would be to show them he was better than they were at something. He found the fastest runner on the team and challenged him to a hundred-yard dash.

"How come you're taking off your shoes, Rube?" someone probably asked, but Billy knew how he ran best. Barefooted, he beat the other man by fifteen feet.

If anyone had asked Billy how he had gotten so fast on his feet, he would have told them the same story he told later in life.

He had been a delicate and sickly baby. Until he was two, Billy's mother had carried him everywhere on a pillow. He could barely walk by the time he was three.

There were no doctors living near the Sundays, but doctors would travel around the country,

14

stopping their teams and wagons at each cabin and asking, "Is anyone sick here?" Then they would treat the person and move on.

One day a Frenchman, a Dr. Avery, came to the Sunday cabin. Billy's mother told him how Billy had been sickly all his life and still could hardly walk.

The old doctor looked Billy over carefully. "I can cure that boy," he told Billy's mother.

"How much will you charge?" Mrs. Sunday asked, thinking of how little money she had.

"If you will feed me and my old mare, that will pay the bill," was the doctor's reply.

The doctor went into the woods and picked leaves from various shrubs, including mulberry leaves, and elderberries. He dug up roots, too, and made a syrup from it all, and gave orders to give it to Billy. The mixture cured Billy, and he ate elderberries and mulberries from then on.

As a baseball player, Billy was not a star, although he played on a team with some of the best players of that day. In his first thirteen times at bat, Billy struck out thirteen times. Even "Cap" Anson had to admit he was a far better fielder than batter.

Because of his poor hitting, Billy was not used in every game, but the crowds liked him because his base stealing made the game more exciting. One year Billy stole ninety-five bases, a record at that time. He could also circle the bases from a standing start in just fourteen seconds.

His batting did not improve much; although he batted .359 for a season, his lifetime average was only .259.

The Whitestocking players were a hard-drinking, quick-to-fight, swearing lot of men, and Billy could hold his own with any of them. His grandfather Corey had been a hard drinker and curser too, although he had tried to keep Billy from following his example. Despite being a professional baseball player and "wild," Billy was known for being honest and perhaps not quite as bad as some of his teammates.

Chicago lost the pennant in 1883 and 1884 to Boston and Providence, but they won it again in 1885. That year marked another major event in Billy's life.

Between the ball grounds and the hotel where Billy lived was the Jefferson Park Presbyterian Church. Billy had passed it many times, but one night he went to a Christian Endeavor youth meeting there. At this meeting he was introduced to Helen Amelia Thompson, called "Nell" by her friends. She was eighteen then, six years younger than Billy, and had accepted the Lord as her Savior when she was fourteen.

Billy looked at the dark-haired girl with the flashing black eyes and said to himself, "There's a swell girl." It was a high compliment, although not in the accepted language of the times.

Billy began attending that church whenever the Whitestockings were in town, and going to the youth meetings too. It took a few weeks for him to get up enough courage to ask Nell, ''Could I see you home?''

Nell hesitated a minute, then smiled and said, ''Yes.''

Actually, Nell only lived across the street from the church. Her father owned the largest dairy and ice cream business in the city at that time. Like Billy's father, he had seen action in the Civil War, and had been badly wounded at the Battle of Shiloh.

Billy may have liked Nell, but there were problems. Nell had a boy friend already; she wanted Billy to date a friend of hers. Billy refused, but he began to attend prayer meetings at the church, sitting along the wall where he could keep one eye on Nell and the other on the preacher.

Billy passed the Thompson house on his way to practice at 10 a.m., again when he went back to the hotel for lunch at noon, once more when he went back for the game in the afternoon, and for the last time when he returned to the hotel for supper.

After a time, Nell began to sweep the Thompson's front steps when she knew Billy would be coming, sometimes sweeping them several times if the game went into extra innings. Billy always stopped to tell her what had happened in that afternoon's game.

The Thompsons were not happy at the idea of their daughter being so friendly with a hard-drinking, swearing, unconverted baseball player, though.

One Sunday afternoon in 1886 Billy went with some of his teammates to a Chicago saloon and drank heavily with them. Later, they walked to a corner and sat down. A wagon was parked there, filled with men and women, some playing cornets and trombones, and singing the old gospel hymns Billy remembered his mother singing in the old log cabin when he was a small child.

The others were watching mostly from curiosity, but Billy had to turn his head to hide his tears. When the music was over, a man stood up and began to talk to them.

"Don't you men want to hear the story of men who used to be dips (pickpockets), yeggs (safe crackers), burglars, second-story workers, drunkards, and have done time in the big house, and who today are sober, honest, have good homes, and are trusted and respected; of women who would sell their womanhood to whoever would buy, were slaves to dope and drink, and now are married and have children of their own?"

The speaker was Harry Monroe, a gambler and passer of counterfeit money before he became a Christian. Now he was the superintendent of the Pacific Garden Mission in Chicago.

"Come down to the Mission and hear stories of redeemed lives that will stir you, no matter whether you have ever been inside of a church or have wandered away from God and decency," Mr.

Monroe went on.

Billy turned to the players who were with him. "Boys," he said, "I bid the old life goodby."

Some of the others smiled, some laughed, some shrugged their shoulders, and some looked at him in disgust. But Billy went to the Mission that night.

Billy did not go forward that first night to accept Jesus as his Savior. He went back to the Mission again and again, though. Finally, partly through the influence of motherly Mrs. Clark, wife of the Mission founder, Billy did go forward to publicly accept Christ as Savior. He would later tell about the experience in detail, even mentioning that there was a knot hole in the board he knelt on that night . . . , and for the rest of his life whenever Billy passed the corner where he had first heard the Mission singers, he stopped to take off his hat and pray his thanks to God.

Billy immediately joined the Jefferson Park Church. Then the press found out about the baseball player who had "gotten religion" and printed their comments. Billy dreaded going to the ball grounds for practice for fear his teammates would laugh at him.

But the first man to meet him that day was Mike "King" Kelly, one of the sport's best players. "Bill, I ain't long on religion, but if old Kell can help you, let me know."

Cap Anson and the others came individually to shake Billy's hand, and his teammates accepted him and his decision.

That day the Whitestockings were playing in Detroit. They were leading when, in the last of the ninth, Detroit had two men on base with two out and Charley Bennett at bat. Bennett hit a long fly to right field where Billy was playing.

"Oh, God," Billy prayed his first prayer on the ball diamond after becoming a Christian. "If ever you helped mortal man in your life, help me get that ball—and you haven't much time to decide."

Billy ran into the crowd that had overflowed onto the field, jumped over a bench, and stopped. He thought he was under the ball, but quickly saw it was going over his head. He jumped, stuck out his left hand, and the ball hit and stuck. Billy was convinced that God had helped him that day because he had taken the first step to turning his life around.

Billy's life did change—in ways everyone could see. He stopped drinking, swearing, gambling, and going to theaters. He refused to play baseball on Sundays.

Instead, he gave talks at the Y.M.C.A. wherever the team was. The boys came to hear about baseball, but Billy told them about finding Jesus.

Jesus had changed Billy Sunday's lifestyle, all right, and everything was going well except for one thing. He had not made much progress with Nell.

3

MARRIAGE

ON New Year's night, 1888, Billy went to see Nell. He thought she looked especially beautiful that night in an ox-blood color cashmere dress and a natural-colored lynx neckpiece her parents had given her for Christmas.

Nell had broken up with her other "beau," and Billy had stopped writing to a girl back in Iowa he had kept in touch with. Both of them were free. Just before midnight Billy decided it was time to ask the question.

"Nell, will you marry me?"

This time Nell did not hesitate with her answer. She came back immediately, "Yes, with all my heart!"

That night Billy did not sleep for happiness, but Mr. Thompson was irate. No daughter of his was going to marry a ball player! Even if he was a Christian, he was still a ball player!

That spring, with Mr. Thompson still refusing to allow the marriage, Billy was sold to the Pittsburgh baseball club. He did not have to go if he didn't want to, however.

Cap Anson and Mr. Spalding both talked to him.

"Billy, you can stay here if you want to," they

told him, "but Pittsburgh will pay you a big increase in salary."

Nell and Billy talked it over. They were agreed Billy should stay in baseball for now, and this looked like a good move for him. He agreed to go to Pittsburgh to play.

Billy had saved $700, and he began to save all he could from his new salary. By September he had sent $1200 back to Nell to bank toward their marriage.

Mr. Thompson might never have given his consent to the marriage, but the young lovers had Mrs. Thompson on their side. She liked Billy and knew Nell loved him, ball player or not. Eventually, in July, Mr. Thompson gave in to her arguments.

Nell wired Billy who was playing in Philadelphia: "Dad says it's all right." That afternoon Billy got three hits and had five put-outs!

Billy and Nell were married at 2 p.m. on September 5, 1888 by Dr. David C. Marquis of the McCormick Theological Seminary in Chicago.

Billy had left the team in Indianapolis the night before, after the game there, to go to Chicago for his wedding. Mr. Spalding had a box at the Chicago field draped for the couple, and asked them to come down before they left for Pittsburgh.

It was a surprise for the newlyweds. The fans in the grandstand and bleachers stood up to cheer them, and Billy's old teammates lined up in front of the Sundays' box, took off their hats, and wished them happiness and long life.

At 5 p.m. the couple left on the Pennsylvania Limited train for the start of their married life.

Marriage was not easy for ball players and their wives. The teams spent a lot of time away from home, on the road, playing in other cities. They were allowed to bring their wives with them on these out-of-town trips, but they had to pay the bills themselves. As a result, most wives did not go with their husbands.

Billy and Nell had an advantage. While Mr. Thompson was not rich, he had enough money, and he often paid Nell's expenses so she could go with Billy. Even so, she spent more than half the time during the season alone at home.

Billy wanted to improve himself through education. He decided to get more training during the winters by going to Northwestern University. Since he did not have the requirements to start college, he made a deal with Northwestern officials. He would coach the college baseball team if they would let him enroll as a special student at their preparatory school, Evanston Academy. This only lasted one winter, but that winter included a course in "rhetoric" where Billy learned the proper enunciation and flourishes considered necessary for any good speaker. It was a course that would come in handy in a few years.

The next year Billy began taking Bible courses at the Chicago Y.M.C.A. He was such an eager student that the director asked him to work permanently for the Y.

It must have taken a lot of "guts" to ask a professional baseball player to give up his career, and Billy did not accept the Y's offer. But in the winter of 1890-91 he worked at the Y again.

Billy felt more and more that he was being called to go into Christian work, but he had been sold by Pittsburgh to Philadelphia for $1000, and had just signed a three-year contract with them. He decided to ask the Philadelphia team to release him from his contract. They refused.

The problem bothered Billy, and he took it to God, asking for a sign of what to do.

"Lord," Billy prayed, "if I don't get my release by March 25th, I will take that as assurance you want me to continue to play ball; if I get it before that date I will accept that as evidence you want me to quit playing ball and go into Christian work."

The release came through on March 17, a little more than a week before Billy's deadline. But with it came another problem. The Cincinnati team, hearing about his release, offered Billy $500 a month for the season. His Y salary would be only $83.33 a month.

Billy had more financial obligations than when he had started playing baseball. His mother had remarried for the third time, but the Sundays now had a year-old daughter, Helen. Billy also had to pay for the care of his brother Albert, still in the mental hospital.

"Is it fair to them and to Nell to give up this

offer?'' Billy asked two of his friends; these were Cyrus McCormick, president of the Y, and J.V. Farwell, a wealthy trustee.

But Billy's answer did not come from them; it came from Nell.

''There is nothing to consider,'' she said firmly. ''You promised God to quit.''

Billy quit. His new job at the Y was as assistant secretary of the religious department. His hours were from 8 a.m. to 10 p.m., six days a week. He had little money now, so he walked to and from work every day, skipped lunch, and had his old clothes made over and dyed to look like they were new.

Billy's work itself was distributing tracts in saloons, giving talks on street corners, leading prayer meetings, and generally trying to help the ''down and outers'' to find salvation, jobs, and a new way of life. Because of his own backgrounds before he was saved, Billy could understand and talk to the men who were victims of liquor and other forces they could not resist.

Despite the long hours, Billy loved his work. For each of the next two years his salary was raised. While it didn't come close to what he could have made playing baseball, it helped meet his bills.

Then, in 1893, came a depression. The Y, which depended on gifts from private citizens to keep going, began to get less money because there was less to give. Billy's salary often wasn't paid on time, making money a problem for him and Nell again.

About this time several people who knew Billy and his Y work suggested his name to the well-known evangelist J. Wilbur Chapman as a good man to assist him in his meetings. Billy was offered $40 a week to join Dr. Chapman.

Just as he had when he had to decide whether or not to give up baseball, Billy took this new offer to the Lord. He knew there was no question about the value and importance of Dr. Chapman's work.

"It would mean reaching more people for Christ than I can in Chicago," Billy thought. Dr. Chapman's meetings covered cities around the country, not just one small area.

Billy gave up his Y work, and although he probably didn't realize it at the time he joined Dr. Chapman, Billy Sunday had taken the first step toward the work that would make his name famous around the world, introduce him to presidents and movie stars, and lead more than one million people to Jesus.

4

AIDE TO J. WILBUR CHAPMAN

BILLY joined John Wilbur Chapman and his team in 1893. Dr. Chapman was a respected revivalist of the day. He had been born in Indiana, and graduated from Oberlin College and Lane Seminary. He was three years older than Billy and was a cultured, earnest man. His preaching was calm, never coarse, but always forceful.

Working beside Dr. Chapman, Billy may truly have felt like the "rube of rubes" he called himself later. Billy's background was that of a tough, hard working, professional ball player. He did not have a college education, and his conversations were filled with slang and expressions from his farm and athletic experiences.

Dr. Chapman, though, apparently saw something in Billy Sunday that not even Billy or Nell had understood. As the advance man, Billy's job was almost as important as the evangelist's. The success of the revival in leading people to Christ depended a great deal on how well it had been set up.

As the advance man, Billy went to the town ahead of the revival. He had to make sure everything was ready for Dr. Chapman. Billy took care of all the details. The most important arrangements he made were to make sure there was enough money to pay for renting a building and advertising. The building had to be big enough to hold the crowds expected.

Billy also worked with the local ministers and volunteer workers from the churches. He helped them set up committees to cover every part of the revival. There had to be a choir committee, an ushers committee, a prayer meeting committee, a publicity committee, a finance committee, and a personal workers committee. There were other, smaller committees, too.

Billy did not mind the long hours he had to spend working with the different committees. What he did mind was being away from home for the two weeks or more that it took to get a revival organized.

The revival actually began when Dr. Chapman and the others arrived. Then Billy became a "jack of all trades." He did whatever was necessary to keep things running smoothly. He was the head usher, he led prayer meetings, he erected tents, he sold copies of Dr. Chapman's books, and now and then was a personal worker.

The one thing Billy did not want to do, though, was speak or preach to the whole congregation. He did not mind talking to individuals or small groups; he was used to that from his Y work in Chicago.

One night in Urbana, Ohio, Dr. Chapman asked Billy to speak. Dr. Chapman was trying to train

Billy.

"I can't speak; I'm not the man for the place," Billy protested. The idea of preaching to so many people frightened him, and he tried to stay away from meetings where he might have to speak to sizable groups.

Billy worked with Dr. Chapman from 1893 to 1895. The revivals were usually in small cities of the Midwest: cities like Peoria, Illinois, and Ft. Wayne, Indiana. Chapman was invited sometimes to larger cities like Brooklyn and Boston, but these meetings were in small neighborhoods. Since they were not all-city, the crowds were not much larger than those in the smaller cities.

These were happy years for "Daddy" and "Ma," as Billy and Nell now called each other. Then, while the Sundays were in Chicago for the Christmas holidays in 1895, Billy got a telegram from Dr. Chapman.

The message from the evangelist was short and to the point. He had decided to give up revivals, at least for now, and become the minister of the Bethany Presbyterian Church in Philadelphia. This was John Wanamaker's church; the merchant had become both a friend and financial supporter of Dr. Chapman, and later Billy would have his support, too.

Again Billy and Nell had no money and no job. The big difference now was that there were two children to be fed and taken care of. Again Billy and Nell prayed, asking God to lead them the way

He wanted them to go.

"Maybe I should go back to play baseball," Billy said. He knew he could still play in the big leagues, and the little bit of money he had been able to save would not last long.

The answer to the Sundays' prayers came a few days later. It was a letter from the ministers in the town of Garner, Iowa. They were asking Billy to come and lead a revival in their town.

Billy and Nell were completely surprised by the request. Why would these ministers decide to invite Billy to hold a revival? They did not know anyone in Garner. Billy had no reputation as a preacher. It was only later that they found out that Dr. Chapman had asked the Garner people to invite Billy when Dr. Chapman had to turn them down himself.

It was not easy for Billy to agree to go on his own, though. There were several big problems. Billy had never led a complete revival himself. He had no staff, no advance preparations, and worst of all, no sermons to preach.

"How can I preach?" Billy asked himself. The only speech he had ever given was one he had used many times with small groups over the years. It was his personal story.

Again Dr. Chapman came to his rescue. "Make use of anything you have heard me say," he told Billy. Then he gave the new evangelist seven of his sermon outlines.

Using the outlines and ideas of other evangelists

was not considered wrong but a way to share in spreading the gospel. Each man put his own personal emphasis and stamp on the stories and examples.

In later years Billy would be criticized by some people for using others' ideas, and he had to have his own sermons copyrighted for protection.

Now, though, Billy was thinking fast about Garner. "If we skip Saturday," he figured, "we can last a maximum of ten days." He accepted the invitation.

Garner was a small town in central Iowa. It had about 1000 people and four churches. One of these was Roman Catholic, but the three Protestant churches were working together to sponsor Billy's revival. They raised enough money to rent the town opera house for a week. The auditorium had seats for 200; the committee hoped that many would come.

When the Garner newspaper wrote about the upcoming revival, Billy was referred to as "W. A. Sunday" instead of "Billy Sunday." It was not until the paper in the next town made the connection between "W. A." and "Billy" that people knew this was the man who had played baseball with the Chicago Whitestockings and Cap Anson. This newspaper gave Billy its wholehearted support. It was the best publicity the revival could have had.

When Billy got to Garner he found a choir of twenty church volunteers, ready to sing. But no song leader.

"I'll lead the singing myself," Billy declared. Later he admitted, "I did not know a note from a horsefly."

Billy preached every evening at 7:30 and held a sunrise service at 7 a.m. Sunday. He was using Dr. Chapman's sermon outlines, and he tried to do things the same way he had seen Dr. Chapman do them for the last three years.

Billy even dressed the way Dr. Chapman had. He wore a wing collar, bow tie, and white waistcoat. He parted his hair in the center to try to cover his receding hairline. He did all he could to keep up the dignity Dr. Chapman had. Billy also tried to correct his own bad grammar and to use less slang when he preached.

On the last night of the Garner revival a special "thank offering" was taken. It came to $68, and was the only pay Billy got.

Even with all the problems in this first Billy Sunday revival, the Lord moved more than 100 people to give their lives to God and fill out a decision card.

Billy used the same kind of decision cards that Dr. Chapman had used. They read, "I have an honest desire henceforth to live a Christian life. I am willing to follow any light God may give me. I ask the people of God to pray for me."

People converted at the meetings signed these cards with their names, addresses, church (or pastor) preferred, and the name of the usher who had been in charge of their section of the auditorium during the service.

Garner was the first of the many revivals Billy Sunday would lead during his life. It was the seed that would grow into a harvest of a million converts for Jesus.

5

UNCONVENTIONAL EVANGELIST

IF Billy had had any doubts about what the Lord wanted him to do with the rest of his life, the success of the revival at Garner should have reassured him. Even before he left the small town Billy had an invitation to preach another revival, at Sigourney, Iowa. From then on, for the rest of his life, Billy Sunday was never without an invitation to preach. Many times he had far more requests than he could handle.

There was one important improvement to the Sigourney revival. Maybe the ministers had heard about Billy's lack of ability as a song leader, because they hired a "songster." Billy would not have to lead the singing this time!

The meetings of this revival were held in the churches who were cooperating on the meetings, except for the one on Sunday afternoon. It was in the courthouse.

In its Janury 23, 1896 issue, the *Signourney News* summed up Billy and the revival. "He talks sound sense and has a way about him that people admire," the reporter wrote.

If Billy was getting homesick for Chicago and his family, he kept it to himself. He went on to five towns before going home.

During the next five years Billy held sixty revivals in small Midwest towns. He carefully went along with the solemn and sacred tone of the services that was traditional. He cooperated with the local ministers and had them preach in their own churches on Sunday mornings.

The congregations at Billy's meetings were often bigger than the population of the whole town. Farm people from around the area came in each evening for the services. Billy began to stay two weeks instead of ten days, and then three weeks, and by 1900 he was holding four-week revivals in most places. His audiences came to hear him again and again. If Billy had had more sermons and less invitations to go somewhere else, he might have stayed for months in one town.

Before 1900 most of Billy's revivals were in Iowa. He did go to towns in Illinois, Indiana, Minnesota, Nebraska, Wisconsin, and Missouri, though. Someone suggested that his revivals seemed to follow the railroad tracks, with a revival at every stop.

The meetings were held in church buildings when the churches were large enough. If they were too small, the local opera house was usually the second choice. Collections were taken to pay to rent the hall, but there was no pressure to give. Nothing was on sale at these meetings—something that would change later, when Billy became more popular.

The free will or "thank offering" was taken the

last day of the revival. This was the only payment Billy got, and often it was very small. In one town a two-week revival brought 127 people to accept the Lord, but the final offering for Billy was only $33.

Billy had no staff of his own to pay, but his personal travel expenses were not considered part of the revival expenses. Billy had to pay his own way to and from the revival town. He had no living expenses while he was there, of course, because he would stay with one of the pastors or a church member.

By 1898, though, most of the little towns did not have a church or any other building big enough for Billy's meetings. He decided to use tents, the way Dr. Chapman had sometimes done. These tents were big, and were put up in a vacant lot as near the center of town as possible to make it easy for everyone to get there.

The churches paid to rent the tent, but Billy had to put it up and take care of it. He kept a lantern in his room so that in case of rain he could hurry down and loosen the tent ropes. Since rain contracts canvas and rope, if he did not loosen them in a storm, the tent would get so tight it would pull up the stakes and collapse. Billy spent quite a few nights sitting up watching the tent.

Tents had other disadvantages.

"They're all right for summer," Billy argued, "but not for cold weather."

Since most revivals were held in the winter, Billy

got little argument. He decided to require a wooden tabernacle for his meetings instead of using tents.

The first tabernacle was built in Perry, Iowa, in 1901. It had 2000 seats and was made completely of wood. It was a simple oblong style. It looked a little like the early Christian churches. There were no decorations inside at all, and outside there was only the banner announcing the meetings.

Even the roof of the tabernacle was wood, covered with tar paper. The walls were made by nailing pine boards to the upright poles that supported the building. For safety, in case of a fire or sudden panic, only two nails were put in each board. That way the crowd could easily tear them off to get out. There were double barn doors at the end of each aisle and cross aisle, so there were plenty of exits.

Inside, the tabernacle had pine benches with no backs, placed in rows. At the front was the platform. It was about five feet high and twenty feet long. In the center was the small pulpit, and the choir and piano were at the back of the platform.

When the first service was held in the tabernacle, Billy knew something had to be done about the wooden floor.

"It was too noisy!" he said. There had been a constant scuffling of feet during the service.

Everyone agreed with him. A few even added

that the floor was also too dusty.

"What can we do about it?" someone asked.

"Cover it with sawdust," Billy decided.

When the news of what Billy was planning got to the local fire fighters, they were quick to complain.

"It's too dangerous to have a building like that with sawdust floors heated with pot bellied stoves," they ruled.

Billy took them to the tabernacle, got a shovel, and scattered red hot coals over the floor to prove the sawdust would not catch fire. The officials were convinced, and from then on the floors of all Billy's tabernacles were covered with sawdust.

The sawdust floors led to the popular expression "Hitting the sawdust trail." This meant, whoever wanted to go forward to confess Jesus walked down a "trail" of sawdust.

Later, however, Nell explained that the expression had originally come from the lumberjacks of the Northwest. The men who had to go into the forest to scale the timber dropped handfuls of sawdust as they went from one spot to another. When they were finished for the day, they said something like, "Now if I can find that sawdust trail I'll be safe and get home." Most people thought the two "sawdust trails" had a lot in common since the one in Billy's tabernacle led "home" to Christ.

The sawdust became a trademark, and it had other advantages. In the busiest years of Billy's

ministry the sawdust used in the big city tabernacles would be sold after the meetings, then sifted
for the coins dropped and lost when the collections
were taken.

In one Iowa town a man came up to Billy after
the services and spread a large cloth on the
platform.

"I'd like a lot of the shavings and sawdust,"
he told Billy. "I want to make a sofa pillow. Right
here is where I knelt down and was converted, and
my wife and four children and my neighbors. I
want to have enough to make a sofa pillow to have
something in my home to help me think of God.
I don't want to forget God or that I was saved.
Can you give me enough?"

"Take enough to make a mattress!" Billy said.
"And if you want enough of the tent to make a
pair of breeches for each boy, take your scissors
and cut it right out if it will help keep your mind
on God."

The Perry tabernacle cost between $700 and
$750, which was a lot of money in those days. The
church members who gave the money got some
of it back, though, by reselling the lumber after
the taberancle was torn down.

Billy's wisdom in using wooden buildings
instead of canvas tents whenever he could was
proved in October, 1905, in Salida, Colorado. On
the last day of the revival a big snowstorm started.

"Give ten men long poles with boards on the
end, and have them push and pull the snow from

the tent top,'' Billy ordered.

Unfortunately, the snow came down faster than the men could clear it from the surface. It finally was piled three feet deep on the tent, and both the center and side poles broke. The tent was torn to ribbons. The revival's final meeting had to be moved to the opera house.

Billy had started his revival ministry with no staff, but he soon saw he had to have help. He had hired local "songsters" along the way, but found his own in 1900. Nell also began to help directly. She eventually became Billy's business manager, and even before she had the job officially she helped with the finances. She later said she had often listened to as many as five sermons a day, and had averaged two a day for forty years.

Around 1900 Billy began to change his style of preaching. Until then he had tried to be as dignified as Dr. Chapman and the more conservative ministers who sponsored him in a town. Perhaps Billy realized that although he could dress like these men, and even imitate them from the pulpit, he was NOT any of them. He was Billy Sunday—orphan, farm boy, former baseball player. He may have seen that he had to start being himself and not a copy of someone else.

In the pulpit Billy began to relax and become just plain Billy Sunday. He had a gift for acting and mimicking, and he began to use it for the Lord. Both his sermons and style of delivery changed.

Billy started caring more about getting a crowd and less about his grammar and dignity. He began to talk like Billy Sunday, not the more sedate Dr. Chapman. Gradually he developed a style of preaching that was as popular with the people as it was sensational.

The Jefferson newspaper, the *Bee*, summed up Billy's meetings and the man himself. "He is not conventional. . . . He is not dull. . . . He is not afraid to wave his hands and shout."

Billy began using slang in his sermons, and in his prayers too. He knew the average person used slang when he talked. Billy wanted everyone to understand what he was saying. He told his audiences that he was a "rube of the rubes," referring to his farm background. Since most of his listeners were either farmers or had been raised on a farm, they knew what he was talking about.

On opening night Billy often said, "Exercise good country cow sense and we'll get along all right. There'll be in my sermons good fodder and rock salt, barbed wire and dynamite."

Billy started preaching more sensationally, too. He acted out sound effects, including a train race that went on for ten minutes. He began to pound the floor or the pulpit. He also pounded the re-inforced wooden chair that he sat on before he began to speak.

He even stood on the pulpit or the chair, and sometimes both! Standing with one foot on the pulpit and one on the chair, Billy would wait until the right moment. Then he emphasized what he was saying by jumping down onto the platform. He also picked up the chair and swung it around his head. Once it accidently slipped and flew through the air over the cringing newspapermen. Fortunately it landed in the sawdust of the aisle and no one was hurt.

Billy also liked to stand on one leg at the very edge of the stage. He would stick the other leg out behind him, lean forward, and shoot his right arm straight out to point toward someone in the audience. Everyone held his breath, waiting to see if Billy would lose his balance and fall. Once or twice he came close, but he never went down.

Billy did so much running, sliding, jumping, falling, and throwing himself across the platform that it was estimated he did not stay in the same spot for a half minute. Someone figured that Billy walked a mile back and forth during each sermon —about 150 miles in a long campaign! And that was in addition to the other exercise he got.

At the end of a special sermon that Billy gave to "men only" audiences, he reminded them of the funny poem of the day, "Slide, Kelly, Slide." Then Billy ran the full length of the platform and flung himself onto the floor like a ball player hook-sliding into second base.

Leaping up quickly, Billy became the "Great Umpire of the Universe." He would give the "out" signal dramatically, lean down and shout, "You're out, Kelly!"

With so much acting and activity in his meetings, Billy was more than a preacher. He was an entertainer. He often acted out all the parts in skits that ran from five to ten minutes. Some of these were Bible stories, like the Prodigal Son. Others came from his own life as a ball player or a boy on the farm. There were ones about the world as it was then. The way Billy acted them out, the audience felt they were right in the middle of it all.

The result of Billy's unusual preaching style was that his meetings got less formal and conservative than the usual church services. Instead of the "hallelujahs" the people were used to saying in church, they began to applaud Billy.

Billy put his whole self into his preaching, working to the limit of his physical strength. He would start fully dressed, then take off his coat, his collar, and then his vest. He often rolled up his shirt sleeves. As the sermon ended, he put everything back on.

At the end of a sermon Billy was so tired he often had to lean on the pulpit. His voice would be hoarse since he had been shouting to reach the whole audience for the full sermon. His clothes were dripping with sweat. No one could deny that Billy Sunday was giving 100%, physically, mentally and spiritually, to his work for Jesus.

In fact, people watching and listening to Billy often unknowingly ground their teeth or clenched their fists as they squirmed in their seats, imitating Billy's action on the platform.

43

These new and unrestrained methods did not please some of the conservative ministers. Neither did the fact that Billy's converts rarely cried; they were much more likely to be smiling.

"God wants people to be happy," Billy pointed out. He himself was a hearty, healthy, and happy Christian and believed everyone else should be too.

The ministers who complained about Billy's style were voted down by the ones who thought getting a crowd to the meetings was more important than the speaker's dignity on the platform, or his slang in sermons and prayers.

Even though Billy was getting better known and more popular all the time, these criticisms bothered him. He still felt inferior to many of the pastors he worked with in planning and developing his revivals.

"Why don't you ask for ordination as a minister?" Nell asked him.

In those days ministers who wanted to have churches had to be ordained, but evangelists did not. Billy had never had any theological training, and although people sometimes called him "Reverend" he really could not use that title.

"Maybe it would help," Billy agreed. He thought perhaps being a true "reverend" would help him overcome his baseball background, which was still against him in some places and with some people.

Being a "rev," Billy thought, would certainly give him dignity and respect with the ordained ministers who invited him to their towns.

Billy asked to be ordained in the Presbyterian Church. His examination came in 1903 in front of a board of ministers from the Chicago Presbytery.

Billy's knowledge of the Bible had been growing over the years, but he still did not know much about theology and church history.

Billy's theology was simple. "With Christ you are saved; without Him you are lost."

When the men examining him asked a question about theology or church history, Billy had only two answers: "That's too deep for me," or "I'll have to pass that up."

After a few questions like that, with Billy's replies showing he had no idea of the "right" answer, a friend moved that the board skip the rest of the exam and pass Billy. His argument was simple.

"God has used him to win more souls to Christ than all of us combined," he told the others, "and God must have ordained him long before we ever thought of it."

Billy was ordained in the Jefferson Park Presbyterian Church where he had met Nell. The sermon for the service was given by his best friend and former co-worker Dr. Chapman.

Now Billy was officially "The Reverend Mr. Sunday," but he was never called that much, and always referred to himself as "plain old Billy Sunday."

"I don't know any more about theology than a jack rabbit knows about ping-pong, but I'm on my way to Glory," he would say proudly. It was this simple faith that was one of Billy's greatest assets in bringing people to Jesus.

6

GROWING FAME

AFTER 1900 Billy Sunday's career picked up speed and power like a snowball rolling downhill. He was swamped with invitations to hold revivals. Sometimes he was scheduled five years ahead.

The days of Billy's casual, quick arrangements for revivals was over. With so many invitations, he had to make changes in the way he ran things. There had to be more organization to getting ready for a revival.

Billy decided the revivals had to be more uniform from town to town, and it took more time now to work on the details. Billy began to ask for more from the local ministers before he would agree to come to their city.

One of the new demands Billy had to make was about money. He asked that the ministers collect pledges from their church members to cover the expected expenses of the revival. This meant that Billy and his team would never have to leave a town with debts that the churches would have to pay.

Again, he was criticized by people who did not understand why he made this request. Actually, Billy's collections always covered the expenses, as he had expected they would, and the pledges never had to be made good.

Later Billy set three major requirements for towns scheduling him for a revival. The evangelistic Protestant ministers had to all agree to support his coming; they had to build him a wooden tabernacle near the center of town; and they had to have the money guaranteed in advance.

There is no record of Billy ever calling off a revival because the full amount of the guarantee was not raised, and many of the big cities did not give it. If Billy felt there was enough money on hand, and that the backers were behind him, he did not insist on the full money or 100% support.

Billy also felt he should not go to a town where another evangelist had been within the past few years. He asked the local preachers not to preach while the revival was going on. His tent or tabernacle was to be the only "church" open, and his sermons the only ones heard while he was in town.

These demands brought more criticism of Billy, but he just pointed out the number of people who had come to Jesus during his campaigns. He also reminded people that his revivals had brought changes in the towns as a whole. There was no arguing the fact that where Billy Sunday had held a revival, alcohol sales were down and gambling almost eliminated.

Being criticized in word and print didn't bother Billy too much. He knew there would be many who did not understand the reasons behind his requests and methods. In Springfield, Illinois, in 1909, though, the criticism took a very personal touch.

Billy had just begun his first sermon of the revival. He noticed a big, dark-haired man sitting on the front bench. He had his hand inside his coat and was glaring at Billy.

Suddenly the man leaped up, pulling a rawhide whip from under his coat. He ran toward the platform, swinging the whip at Billy's legs and body, shouting, "I have a commission from God to horsewhip you!"

The whip hit Billy twice, and then his quick temper, which he had to fight all his life, boiled. Billy leaped from the platform, reaching for the man and yelling, "Well, I have a commission from God to knock the tar out of you, you lobster!"

The man tried to run back up the aisle, but he was caught by the police stationed there. The police actually had to protect the man from the people in the tabernacle that night.

Billy sprained his ankle in his dramatic leap from the stage. He had to preach the rest of the revival on crutches. When Billy learned that the man had recently been in the state mental hospital, he did not prosecute.

Other than the devil himself, Billy's chief enemy and target was alcohol in any form. This was the day of the saloon, and many men came home drunk at night to beat their wives and children.

Billy vigorously favored Prohibition (making all sales and use of liquor illegal). He attacked the companies that made liquor. In 1905 he preached a sermon that came to be called his "booze sermon." It lasted about an hour and forty minutes, and was one of his most popular. It has been reprinted many times since then.

"I'm trying to make America so dry that a man must be primed before he can spit," Billy said once. "I'm going to fight the liquor business till hell freezes over, and then I'll put on ice skates and fight it some more!"

Naturally the liquor businessmen and companies were not happy with Billy Sunday and his revivals. They fought back. They sent people into the towns before Billy was to come, trying to counter what they knew he would say. These liquor companies spent a lot of money fighting Billy Sunday because it had become common for a town to vote to go "dry" (no liquor sales) after Billy had been there. It was claimed that in one day in Illinois 1,500 saloons were put out of business, mostly because of Billy Sunday.

Although Billy was loudly in favor of Prohibition, he did not join any of the political groups working for it. He never forgot that as far as politics went, he was neutral when he preached.

Billy stayed away from controversial things in his sermons. "It is my business to get men to take a stand for Christ," he said. He left everything else to the regular pastors who would be with these men after Billy left town. He worked only to persuade sinners to accept Christ.

Once a person had filled out his decision card, Billy felt his part of the work was done. The new Christian then belonged to the local minister and the church.

As Billy's fame grew and he got more requests to hold revivals, he had to get a bigger staff. From 1900 to 1918 the people working with Billy increased to twenty-three. Many of these workers were women. Billy believed in allowing women to vote, and showed his support by giving them full status on his team.

Nell, of course, was the top woman. Although the Sundays had three boys and a girl, they spent most of their time at home with grandparents or a nurse. Later they went to boarding schools. Nell spent all the time she could helping Billy. She became his business manager, led prayer meetings, spoke to women's groups, and taught Bible classes when she was needed.

In 1908 Billy hired a new song leader. He was a handsome, dark-haired twenty-eight-year-old bachelor named Homer Rodeheaver. ''Rody,'' as he was better known to everyone, was almost as colorful as Billy.

Rody played a golden trombone and was a genius in getting audiences to sing. Born in Ohio and raised in Tennessee, Rody was a veteran of the Spanish-American War. He would stay with Billy for twenty years—the best and busiest of

51

Billy's career.

Rody agreed with Billy that God wanted people to be happy, not grim. He felt singing was one way to show that happiness. One of the ways Rody got the audience involved in the music was to have the choir sing one line of a hymn, then the last ten rows of people in the back of the tabernacle sang the answering line. Those who heard this effect on the hymn "For You I Am Praying" said it was electrical.

Rody had a fine baritone voice, and could sing solos, duets, or be part of a trio or quartet. He was also an amateur magician and often used these tricks when he led children's meetings.

Rody's chief job, though, was to organize the choirs—sometimes involving thousands of people in the big cities—and have them singing every night of the eight to ten weeks of the revival. These choirs were made up of church choir members and people who just wanted to sing for the Lord in a Billy Sunday meeting. It wasn't easy to make such a variety of singers into a choir in a short time, but Rody did it in city after city.

Rody gave these volunteer singers trained leadership, which they usually had never had, in return for their services. Singing in a Billy Sunday choir led by Homer Rodeheaver was not only a way to serve Christ and community, but also a personal lifetime highlight for many people.

Another member of Billy's staff was Jack Cardiff. Jack had been a serious contender for the welterweight boxing championship when he was converted and joined Billy in 1912. Jack was Billy's personal masseur. Billy worked so hard physically as he preached that he needed a rubdown after every service to help ease his tired body. In 1917 Jack left the team to become pastor of his own church.

As Billy's staff grew he had to ask the towns to give him a furnished house where he and the team could live together during the campaign. Until then, Billy and the others had stayed in private homes or hotels.

Now, though, everyone lived and ate as a family. Billy and Nell sat at the head of the dinner table and listened to reports from each person about his work. Then Billy made his decisions, gave his orders, and set the policies for the job ahead.

Everyone on Billy's staff was a born-again Christian. Each believed God was guiding their work. Still, even with God's guidance they knew there had to be careful planning, and they were convinced that God was using Billy as one of His human agents on earth.

Most of Billy's staff called him "the boss," and did whatever he told them. They liked Billy. He was friendly, easy-going, and generous. He also loved practical jokes. Although Billy lost his temper quickly, he was also quick to forgive and forget.

Nell, on the other hand, was more hardheaded

and businesslike. She worked hard herself and expected everyone else to work just as hard. A few of the staff called her "Ma," the way Billy always did, but most of them called her "Mrs. Sunday," at least when talking to her. The staff appreciated Nell's ability to keep a more practical eye on things than Billy did, but they probably loved him more.

The pace of Billy's life was beginning now to tell physically on him. The nervous excitement of a meeting often kept him awake at night, despite his rubdown.

"The blood in my brain works like a trip hammer," Billy once told an audience as he described what he went through. "When I lie down I go over every sermon that I preach. I preach it all over. I see the faces in front of me."

Billy also often told his listeners, "I never expect to be an old man. I am burning up to keep you out of hell."

From 1908 on, doctors constantly warned Billy that he would have to slow down or he would not live another ten years. He never changed his top-speed pace, though.

Nell did all she could to conserve Billy's strength as the years went by. "My job is to sit on the safety valve," she told reporters once.

Nell made sure no one bothered Billy when he was resting, and he spent much of his little bit of free time resting. She was also the one who insisted he turn his coat collar up to keep his neck and throat warm after a strenuous sermon. And she smoothed things over when Billy's temper upset his staff or others.

Nell had to try to keep Billy from being too generous with his time and money. He often agreed to speak free of charge at outside meetings during his campaigns. Two groups Billy would never turn down were the inmates of local prisons and temperance meetings. He would travel more than 100 miles on his day off just to give his "booze sermon" if he thought it would help bring Prohibition to the country.

Although Billy was now well known in the Midwest, and even had been in *Who's Who in America* in 1903, he was not well known in the big Eastern cities. He got his first national publicity in 1907 when the popular *American Magazine* did a story about his revival in Fairfield, Iowa.

Whether the author of that article meant to make fun of Billy by showing his sensational methods is not known, but the article had the opposite effect on readers. People got curious about Billy, and were more ready to admire him than to laugh at him.

In 1914 the same magazine ran a poll of its readers. "Who is the greatest man in the United States?" was the question. Billy Sunday came in eighth, tied with Andrew Carnegie and Judge Ben Lindsey. Only one other preacher was even mentioned among the thousands of names suggested by readers.

Billy Sunday was no longer "small town and

small time." He was ready now to "invade" the big cities for God.

7

BILLY IN PHILADELPHIA

BILLY'S "big city" campaigns began in the East with Philadelphia in 1915. He went on to Baltimore in 1916, and after revivals in Kansas City and Detroit went on to New York in 1917 and Washington, D.C., in 1918.

By now Billy was *Doctor* William A. Sunday. Westminster College, a United Presbyterian college in New Wilmington, Pennsylvania, had awarded him an honorary Doctor of Divinity (D.D.) degree in 1912. Even with this official title, though, he was still "Billy" to everyone.

The Eastern revivals were from eight to ten weeks long, but the one in Philadelphia went on for eleven weeks.

What was it like to live in a city where Billy Sunday was coming to hold a revival? What was it like to go to one of his services? Let's pretend we are living in Philadelphia when Billy's revival came on January 3 and lasted until March 21, 1915.

Actually, the revival had begun months before the first song or sermon. The invitation had to be sent to Billy by the city's ministers. The starting date had to be set to fit in with Billy's other revivals already scheduled. The tabernacle size and location had to be agreed on. The guarantee fund had to be raised. These problems often took a year to work out.

Once these first steps were settled, Billy's advance man came to town. That was probably about eight months before you went to hear Billy himself.

The advance man for Billy did the same kind of work Billy had done for Dr. Chapman in the 1890s, but on a larger scale. The advance man explained to the churches how many people, and what kind of people, he needed to work before and during the revival. As a church member in the city expecting Billy Sunday, you would probably be given a "work card" where you could put down what work you wanted to do for the revival.

You might offer to be a choir member, an usher, a secretary who would help converts fill out their decision cards, a doorkeeper, a personal worker, an automobile driver (if you had your own car to use), or, if you were a woman, an organizer for the noonday lunches and devotional meetings or a nursery worker. Billy did not allow children under four in the tabernacle, so he began a new service: a nursery for children, held at a nearby church.

As many as 20,000 Christians would be lined up this way, including those who offered to use their homes for "cottage prayer meetings" before and during the revival.

These "cottage prayer meetings" were a vital

part of a Billy Sunday campaign. They were set up with a special system Billy used. The city was divided into districts, and then divided again. In the center of each area was a home where the prayer meetings would be held. Each house holding the meetings was given a sign to put in a front window. Everyone knew exactly where to come, and no one in the entire city was more than a few blocks away from a prayer group.

During the month before the Philadelphia campaign there were home prayer meetings in more than 5,000 homes, two times a week, with about 100,000 people. What a wave of prayer to lift up the Billy Sunday team and the revival!

The tabernacle would be started next, and you could keep a daily eye on its progress as it was built. These were still wooden, except in Boston where the only masonry one was ever built. The tabernacles had changed a lot in size and decoration from the first one back in Perry, Iowa, though.

The roof was flatter now, and called a "turtle back." Dormer windows were built into the roof so that afternoon meetings would have extra light, and save electricity. The bare board walls, the double barn doors, and the long rows of pine benches were the same as ever, except that now the benches had backs on them for comfort. Sometimes, too, the inside of the tabernacle would get a coat of whitewash.

The platform was higher and longer than in the

early days. Now there was a trap door at the front edge of the platform near the pulpit. When Billy was through preaching, he would open this door, slip down into a "well" in the floor, and shake hands more easily with the converts as they came down the aisles past him. The well was about as high as Billy's waist, and as the converts reached up to grip his hand, Billy reached down to them.

The pulpit was part of the platform now. It was built strong enough to be stood on without worrying about whether it would tip or break. The whole platform was covered with carpet to keep down the noise of Billy's always-moving feet.

Noise was a big problem in all the large tabernacles. There was no such thing yet as a loudspeaker, and Billy had to use a sounding board to make himself heard. This was a large board placed behind the pulpit, tipped slightly toward the audience, that was to reflect the words of the speaker back to the listeners.

Even using the sounding board and his own loud voice, it was almost impossible for Billy to make himself heard clearly in the back rows. He often stopped preaching to ask people to be more quiet. Noise was the main reason Billy did not want children in the tabernacle.

Reporters sat at the press tables which were built in level at each end of the platform. They sat facing the audience and had their notebooks on the platform floor. Now and then they had to grab them up quickly to keep the notebooks—and their hands—from being stepped on by Billy.

The Philadelphia tabernacle could seat 18,000 people, and was heated by thirty iron stoves. Special men, trained in using the stoves, were hired to keep them fueled and going.

Hundreds of bare electric light bulbs were strung across the rafters of the tabernacle. They gave a glaring, but bright, light to the room.

The floor, which was still usually the ground, was sloped slightly forward and was covered with truckloads of the famous sawdust.

For the services the platform was draped with bright bunting, and the pulpit had an American flag on it. Above the platform was a big banner "PHILADELPHIA [or whatever city it was] FOR CHRIST." The walls also had banners on them. "SAVED FOR SERVICE" and "GET RIGHT WITH GOD" were two of the mottos. Outside, a banner saying "BILLY SUNDAY TABERNACLE" hung at the front.

The total cost of a big city tabernacle was high. The Philadelphia one cost $24,000, although Billy did all he could to keep costs down. He also claimed to use only union labor in building them. By dividing the total cost by the number of seats, though, a single seat cost only $1 to $1.50. And these seats were filled over and over during the revival.

The New York City tabernacle was the largest of all. It had not only the main room, but also a post office, hospital, rooms for personal workers, ushers and members of the press, plus book rooms and a retiring room for Billy.

You would not be the only one watching as the tabernacle went up. Hundreds of people checked its progress every day as they went to work, and the newspapers covered its building, too. The newspapers were probably Billy's best publicity for the revival coming soon.

The tabernacle was usually dedicated a week before Billy came to the city. This special service was by ticket only, and the tickets were very carefully given out.

One religious newspaper happily called all this "Big business for the Lord." Billy would have agreed.

"God is in the greatest business there is," he said once. "It takes more brains to sell goods than to make them."

The revival was scheduled to begin on a Sunday. Billy arrived Friday evening. You would probably have been one of the thousands of people who met him at the train station. There was an official welcoming committee, brass bands, marching choirs, plus the big hymn-singing crowd. A parade wound through the city, with Billy waving from the back of an open car to the people along the street. Mounted policemen escorted him. Some said Philadelphia gave Billy the biggest welcome it had ever given anyone.

When the parade got to the house where Billy and his staff would stay, there was a reception for him. Billy was introduced to local officials and then interviewed by reporters.

On Saturday morning Billy held a private meeting with the ministers in charge of the revival, and the committee chairmen. He had them meet his staff and gave them his plans and orders for the campaign coming up. There was no doubt that Billy Sunday was the one in charge of the Billy Sunday revival.

The first service of the revival was usually at 10:30 Sunday morning. There would be another at 3 p.m. and a third at 7 p.m.

If you had been going to the Philadelphia meeting that first Sunday morning you would either have had to get to the tabernacle very early or been a member of a special delegation with reserved seats. These delegations were usually Bible classes from the local churches for the first few meetings. People came not only from Philadelphia, but from New York City and all the areas around the city.

As you pushed your way through the crowds near the tabernacle you would have noticed right away how many police were around. Extra police and fire fighters were always needed at Billy's meetings. The police directed the huge crowds and traffic, but they were also there to protect Billy, who often got threatening letters.

Outside and around the tabernacle you would find the anti-Sunday people. They were usually selling some kind of book or pamphlet. The police made sure no one was bothered by these people and that Billy was not heckled when he started speaking.

Twenty minutes after the doors were opened, the 18,000 seats in the tabernacle were filled. While there were women in all the meetings, you would have seen easily that most of the audience were men. Billy Sunday was a man's man. Men were attracted to him because they knew he had lived as hard a life as they had when he was small, and had been a professional athlete. They knew he had been a drinker, fighter, and swearer himself, and that told them Billy understood them.

Billy and his staff did not neglect women, though. There were many daytime meetings that were attended mostly by women. These special meetings were held in homes, factories and shops, and in other buildings.

When the tabernacle was filled, men tried to climb into the rafters, while others got up on the roof, trying to look through the windows. Billy would be interrupted constantly by their shouts and pounding at the door to get in, and the noise of the police chasing them away.

Inside the tabernacle you had a chance to buy pictures of Billy, his biography, or a hymnbook.

Homer Rodeheaver held a half-hour "warm up" song period with the crowd before Billy came to the pulpit. Not only would there be singing, but Rody also told jokes and stories. Some of these he changed to fit the city where the revival was, or were about what was going on in the crowd.

Rody asked the delegations to sing their favorite hymns or songs. Sometimes the delegations were by occupation, and the hymns they sang were loosely, and often humorously, tied to their work. The insurance salesmen once asked for "Blessed Assurance," while a group of laundry workers wanted "Wash Me and I Shall Be Whiter Than Snow."

Rody, with his southern accent and a "polish" Billy would never have, was a favorite with the crowd, especially the women.

The hymns Rody liked to sing were sometimes new ones, and he had to teach the audience the words. Many of these new hymns were ones Rody had written himself. But most of the hymns sung were militant ones like "Onward, Christian Soldiers." The most popular gospel song of Billy's campaigns, though, was "Brighten the Corner Where You Are."

Do not wait until some deed of greatness you
    may do,
Do not wait to shed your light afar;
To the many duties ever near you now be true,
Brighten the corner where you are.

CHORUS: Brighten the corner where you are.
            Brighten the corner where you are.
            Someone far from harbor you may
                guide across the bar,
            Brighten the corner where you are.

Just above are clouded skies that you may
  help to clear;
Let not narrow self your way debar.
Tho into one heart alone may fall your song
  of cheer,
Brighten the corner where you are.

Here for all your talent you may surely find
  a need;
Here reflect the Bright and Morning Star.
Even from your humble hand the bread of life
  may feed,
Brighten the corner where you are.

—Words by Ina Duley Ogdon
© Rodeheaver Music Company

After the singing, when the crowd was already
involved, Billy Sunday came onto the platform.
He sat down at the back, but the applause was
deafening. When Billy began to preach, the tabernacle got quiet, though.

One of the first things Billy did when he started
to preach was to take off his coat. Then he told
the men in the audience to take theirs off, too,
so they could all be confortable.

After a few words of introduction, Billy would
begin the sermon that he used to start every
revival: "Have Ye Received the Holy Spirit?"

Billy may or may not have been what you were
expecting from what you had heard and read

about him. He may have seemed different to you in person. His voice was hoarse and gravelly from the years of straining to make himself heard by the big crowds. He talked as fast as an auctioneer, some said.

A reporter noted that Billy didn't often lower his voice for effect. Instead he often lingered on a word, letting his tone rise almost to a falsetto. The wail that made, the reporter wrote, could penetrate the air outside.

"It is weird," the reporter ended, "but effective."

Billy was often interrupted by laughter and applause as he gave his sermons, acted out all the parts in skits, or moved around the platform. Stenographers trying to take down what he said in shorthand claimed he could talk at three-hundred words a minute.

Whether you were surprised at Billy's voice or not, you had expected to see the leaps, runs, slides, kicks, hops, and shaking fists you had read about. You were not disappointed. What you had read or heard about Billy Sunday and his actions on the platform could not begin to come up to what it was like to see him in person.

Another thing the reporters could not describe for you was how Billy could make you feel close to him when you were really only one of thousands in the tabernacle. "Magnetic" was the only word that fit Billy's gift of making each listener feel he was the only one Billy was talking to. Even those who went forward when the call for converts came felt they were the only one Billy really meant to come up the aisle. When Billy looked directly into your eyes with his blue ones, you were sure he knew you personally when he said, "God bless you."

Billy gave the same sermons at all his revivals, although he added new ones now and then. By the time he got to Philadelphia, he had preached some of them almost a hundred times. Yet Billy always went over every sermon alone before he preached it again.

Sitting in the tabernacle you would not see where Billy's pulpit Bible was open. But it was always open to the same place, no matter what sermon he was preaching or what text he was using. It was always open to Isaiah 61:1. "The spirit of the Lord God is upon me; because the Lord hath anointed me to preach good tidings unto the meek...." This is the same text Jesus read in the synagogue at Nazareth (Luke 4:17-19).

Billy was often criticized for "borrowing" material from others for his sermons. Once he was found to be using part of a Robert Ingersoll speech. Ingersoll was the foremost atheist of the day, so the accusation that he was using Ingersoll's material was doubly hard for Billy to take. He denied ever having read that particular speech, but quickly admitted he had read everything Ingersoll had written that attacked the Bible. Billy wanted to know what the enemy was thinking and saying, but he never used that material again.

Billy tried to explain that he had never used all-original sermons. "I am indebted to various friends of mine for some of my thoughts," he often said, "though I do not always give credit."

In a talk to students preparing for the ministry at the Episcopal Theological Seminary in Cambridge, Massachusetts, Billy once explained how he wrote his sermons:

"I attend to them carefully and have a large envelope for each subject, and in this envelope I put clippings or notes of everything pertinent to it from newspapers, magazines, biographies, or histories, once in a while adding a Bible paragraph. In this way I am increasing my sermons at all times."

Once the first sermon of the campaign was over, the audience moved out. Others came in immediately. Some people brought their lunches and dinners when they came to the first meeting so they could sit all day in the tabernacle and hear all three sermons.

On that first day in Philadelphia you would have learned you had been one of 70,000 to hear Billy— and you would have found out later that half that many were turned away because there was no more room.

For the rest of the campaign Billy would preach every day at 2 and 7 p.m. There were no regular meetings on Mondays. These were supposed to be Billy's days off.

No photographers were allowed in the tabernacle during the services. Their "flashes" would have caused too much distraction. The newspapers who wanted pictures of Billy "in action" sent cartoonists to make sketches as Billy preached. Sometimes Billy gave the paper copies of his sermons in advance, which made it easier for the artists to follow.

If you had been in that Philadelphia audience the first day of Billy's revival, you would not have heard him call listeners to come forward and accept Christ as Savior. Billy never gave a call for converts the first day of a campaign, the way most of the other evangelists did. He waited until after the first week of meetings, usually. That way the suspense grew and the newspapers gave him more publicity. The first call usually came after the eighth day, and when Billy felt the time was just right. His staff knew the first call was likely to come after the sermon "The Hour Is Come."

While there were definitely some very emotional scenes and conversions during Billy's campaigns, he did not aim for that.

"What I want and preach is the fact that a man can be converted without any fuss," he said. "It's an insult to religion to call it emotional. If nothing in religion appeals to a man's intelligence and judgments, he is in a sad way."

Once the call was given, the converts started down the aisles, led by the ushers. Billy opened the trap door and dropped down into the well. The ushers formed the converts into two lines, with one coming toward Billy from each direction. One usher grabbed the right arm of each person coming from one side, and put that person's hand into Billy's right hand. The other usher took the hand of the person coming from the other side and put it into Billy's left hand. Billy was always looking and swinging from right to left and back, quickly. It was said he could shake 57 hands a minute. Even so, Billy was able to make each convert feel special as he gripped his hand and looked into his eyes.

If you had come forward to accept Christ as your Savior and to shake Billy's hand, you would then have been led to the front seats and given a decision card. The secretary who handed it to you would help you fill it out if you needed help. Then she would give you a special brochure Billy had written, and you would be led back to your seat so that other converts could have the front seats.

The brochure you were given had a picture of Billy and a short note from him to the new Christian on the cover. Billy suggested pasting this tract into your Bible so you could read it often.

Inside, the circular was divided into two parts: "What It Means to Be a Christian" and "How to Make a Success of the Christian Life." This last listed seven suggestions for Christian growth. They were: Study the Bible; Pray much; Win someone for Christ; Shun evil companions; Join some church; Give to the support of the Lord's work; Do not become discouraged. Each of these was

71

explained with Bible verses.

Collections were taken at every meeting now, and Billy also asked for pledges. The advance publicity promised that as soon as the expenses of the meetings had been raised, there would be no more collections. It became important to a city to give more on the first day of the revival than any other city had, and the amounts were reported to the newspapers and printed.

Billy often apologized for these collections. He reminded the people that he did not get any of that money himself. Everyone tried hard to get the expenses paid off before the last week of the revival so they would not have to take collections at the final meetings.

During the time Billy was not preaching he was not just sitting around. To reach women who were wealthy and "in society," Billy led "parlor meetings" each Thursday morning. These were in homes of the most important people in the city, and you were invited only by engraved invitation.

At these meetings Billy gave special sermons, without any slang or the gymnastics that were the biggest part of his regular tabernacle meetings. He spoke in the homes of Mrs. Thomas Edison, Mrs. John Rockefeller, Jr., and Mrs. Marshall Fields.

Billy wanted these meetings to be taken seriously. He did not want them to be only "social events." He once asked the women, "Have you ladies accepted Jesus Christ as your Savior? Are you attending these meetings to be benefitted spiritually? I'll quit if you come to see me or to visit beautiful homes or to get a nice ride in your autos.''

In Philadelphia Billy made the newspapers in a different way when he played in an Old Timers baseball game in Shibe Park on St. Patrick's Day. Billy was now fifty-three years old, but he hit a home run and ran around the bases in just sixteen seconds.

By the time Billy and his staff left Philadelphia, more than two million people had heard him speak in the tabernacle, while about one million more had heard someone from his staff in a factory, office, club, or private home. Over 40,000 converts had been registered, with more than 1,800 "hitting the sawdust trail" on the last day.

Billy and his staff moved on to other revivals in other cities, but many years later, in an attempt to see if any of Billy Sunday's influence remained in the city, a survey was made. Though over a generation had passed, it was reported that many Philadelphians traced their faith in Jesus to the witness of someone converted at a Billy Sunday meeting.

Some converts always fell away after a revival, but the majority, according to church records, did not.

8

BIG CITY REVIVALS

FROM Philadelphia Billy and his team went on to revivals scheduled in other big cities. Each one had its own interesting and unique side and highlights.

In Baltimore the newspapers began calling the tabernacle the "Salvation Shed." It was built in front of the Oriole baseball park. On the last night of the campaign there, Billy looked up to see the great baseball star of the day, the Yankee's "Home Run" Baker, coming down the aisle with four of his teammates.

While he was in Baltimore, Billy preached at noon one day to the staff and faculty at Johns Hopkins University Hospital. He told them that Christian physicians should take advantage of their influence with patients to tell them about Jesus.

Detroit was also a "revival city" for Billy. Henry Leland, president of Cadillac, had worked hard to get Billy to come. As a personal thank-offering, Mr. Leland gave Billy a brand new $8000 Cadillac. It was Leland, too, who gave Billy one of his many nicknames. "Great plumed knight," Leland said, "and clothed in the armor of God."

Regardless of what city Billy was preaching in, the newspapers covered every meeting. Many of them printed his whole sermon the next day. To show his gratitude for the reporters' cooperation, Billy visited the editorial offices of every paper that printed the sermons and thanked the writers personally.

Papers also ran special columns of Billy's short sayings. Some called them "Sizzlers from Sunday's Sermons," or "Hot Shots from Billy." In Kansas City one column was headed "Billy Sunday's Epigrammatic Speed Balls as They Rolled Over the Old Home Plate."

Everything Billy said was news and was read eagerly by people in the city. Even those who had been at the meeting the night before and heard the sermon read about it. It was coverage like that that helped make the audience even bigger the next night.

Billy's short sayings were especially popular, and they were easy to pick out of his sermons.

Some of these painted vivid pictures for the listeners. "I'm sick and tired of hearing Jesus pictured as a sort who allowed Himself to be a cuspidor and a doormat. Jesus was the bravest man that ever walked the face of the earth."

Others were humorous. "The time for a man to sow his wild oats is between the ages of eighty-five and ninety." Or "Going to church doesn't make a man a Christian any more than going to a garage makes him an automobile."

Billy's campaigns were successful in all the cities. One Baltimore church took in sixty-five new members one Sunday while Billy was there; eighty-five on another Sunday. Other churches saw much the same results.

Although Billy was no doubt pleased, encouraged, and thankful for so many converts in these cities, it was New York City that he really wanted to preach in. To Billy the biggest city of all was the center of all evil and the enemy of religion. His campaign there would be the biggest, most important of his career. It would run from April 7 to June 17, 1917.

It took a whole year of preparation and at least 20,000 meetings beforehand before the New York City campaign began. The tabernacle was built at 168th and Broadway and could seat 16,000 with standing room for 4,000 more. It cost more than $65,000 to put up.

By the time Billy got to New York, though, two things had happened that made him change some of his ways. The first was America getting into World War I on April 6, 1917. The second thing was the battle being fought in the newspapers, and sometimes in the churches, about Billy and the money he was personally getting from the "thank offerings" after each revival.

The war had begun in Europe in 1914, and Billy had taken the same attitude that most Americans had. Europe was far away, and the countries there always seemed to be fighting over something. There was no reason for the United States, many miles of ocean away, to worry about the war or get into it. Billy, like many others of his time, was not even sure which side was the "right" side. Until the United States actually declared war on Germany and her allies, Billy rarely mentioned the war in either his sermons or interviews with reporters.

The matter of the money was something else. It was against Billy personally. The thank offerings had been getting larger over the years, and the newspapers told everyone all the figures. Billy now owned an apple ranch in Hood River, Oregon, as well as his home in Winona Lake, Indiana. Winona Lake was the site of the Winona Lake Bible Conference each year, begun by Dr. Chapman in the late 1890's. The Sundays had started spending their summers there in the early 1900's and had built a bungalow overlooking the lake in 1910.

Often when Billy came back to Winona Lake for a visit or vacation, his neighbors would meet him at the train station with a loud welcome. He felt truly "at home" there.

Billy was also active in the Interdenominational Association of Evangelists which had been started at Winona Lake in 1904. This group gave evangelists a chance to meet and visit and to exchange ideas and discuss new techniques.

The critics of Billy's personal income and his owning two properties did not consider that he paid part of his staff's expenses out of his own money, or that he tithed all he received, giving it to charity.

Nor did the critics take into account the location of Winona Lake. It is in the northern part of Indiana, and then was just south of a major highway. It was only two hours from Chicago, and a perfect place for a man who traveled all over the country to live, but it was not the ideal place for relaxation.

Billy spent about half his summer on the ranch in Oregon and half at Winona Lake. It was only in Oregon, though, that he was able to completely relax and rest for the next season's revivals. There were too many other things he was involved in when he was at Winona Lake. This made it hard for him to do much relaxing there.

The newspapers not only printed how much money Billy was given at the end of each revival, but they were also suggesting that he and his staff were using "polite blackmail" to get contributions. There was no problem finding people willing to back them up on this charge.

This attack could not go unchallenged if Billy Sunday was to come to New York City. John D. Rockefeller, Jr. hired a private investigator to check the facts.

Mr. Rockefeller reported the results in the *New York World*. "I studied Mr. Sunday's financial methods, and I found that no effort was made anywhere to get contributions. The people whom he helped gave what they felt like giving. No one was asked to give a cent."

Billy was not satisfied with this, though. During his very first sermon in New York he suddenly stopped talking. As the surprised crowd waited, Billy told them he had been called "a grafter" for the money he made, but the entire offering given him at the end of this campaign would go to the Red Cross and to the war work of the Y.M.C.A.

Later, in Chicago, Billy gave the entire thank offering to the Pacific Garden Mission where he had found the Lord himself years before.

Once America was actually in the war, Billy exemplified patriotism and did all he could personally to help the government and the war effort. He tried to reach as many men in uniform as he could before they shipped out for France and the fighting. Billy preached at military posts all over the country, urging those in the armed forces to be soldiers of Jesus Christ.

Billy's sermons took on a patriotic tone, too. He urged Americans to help in every way they could. He personally sold millions of dollars worth of Liberty Bonds, which were sold to help finance the war.

At least once Billy's powerful preaching against the German Kaiser brought a personal attack again. A German-American, angry at Billy's remarks, went after him with a whip. Billy was not hurt and kept up his anti-German preaching.

In the spring of 1918 Billy planned to go to France to preach to the men in the trenches. Before he could make his final plans, however, he got a call from President Wilson to come to the White House.

Billy had been to the White House before, but he was surprised at the reason for this visit. President Wilson wanted him to put off his trip to Europe.

"I believe there are enough speakers, singers, and entertainers overseas," the President told Billy. "I would like you to stay home and go from city to city." Mr. Wilson believed Billy could get more Americans to work harder and do more for the war that way. He felt that would help win the war sooner than if Billy went to preach to the soldiers.

Billy was disappointed, but as a patriotic citizen he had no choice but to obey his leader. "Mr. President, your wish is law with me," Billy said, and canceled his plans.

Sometimes the shortages that the war brought were a problem to Billy and the committees working to set up a revival. In Providence, Rhode Island, in the fall of 1918, the Federal Priorities Division of the War Industries Board declared that material for building Billy's tabernacle in that city would not be considered a "priority" for the war effort.

Fortunately, the committee was able to find enough lumber to build the tabernacle anyway, but two weeks after Billy began the campaign the Spanish influenza hit. The epidemic was so bad that the state health authorities had to close all theaters, schools, churches, and the Billy Sunday meetings.

In early 1918 Billy brought his campaign to Washington, D.C. The tabernacle was built on government property just a few blocks from the Capital and the Union Station.

During his stay in the capital, Billy was asked to give the prayer at the opening session of Congress on January 10. It was probably the most unusual prayer ever given in the House of Representatives. It was a praise of America and its war effort, and was interruped three times by applause!

World War I ended on November 11, 1918. There was jubilation and celebration across the country at the end of the killing. In the midst of this happy time, however, few people realized that an era had ended, as well as a war. The twentieth century was finally here, and it would change the world, the United States, and Billy Sunday's kind of revival.

9

THE CHANGING MOOD

AFTER the hardships and worries of World
War I were over, the mood of the American
people changed. They were ready for fun. They
did not want to be told they were sinners; that was
not fun!

The churches went along with the temper of the
times. Joining a church became the social thing
to do. Almost all the churches who had sponsored
Billy Sunday and other revivalists were now
divided into "Modern" and "Fundamental" sides.
The fight to see which side would control the
churches was hottest in the early 1920's.

Billy sided with the Fundamentalists. This meant
that in some places the other side saw his revival
more as a move by the Fundamentalists to get control of the church than as a religious campaign to
win people to Christ. They were often against
inviting Billy at all.

Billy had come to the end of one big battle: Prohibition had won. The Eighteenth Amendment to
the Constitution was ratified by the states on
January 16, 1919. Liquor could no longer be
bought, sold, or used in the United States. It had
been voted overwhelmingly by the state legis-
latures. Billy was openly given credit for doing

more than anyone else to bring the people to the point of demanding this new law.

With Prohibition a fact, Billy found the people were tired of professional evangelism. They had other ways to have fun now, too. The movies, radio, and the automobile were now common, and gave them a better time than tabernacle meetings had.

To make matters worse for Billy, there had been a lot of people trying to copy his methods in revivals. But Billy Sunday was impossible to copy. Many of those who tried ended up looking silly, and making the churches who had invited them look bad too. These "copycat" evangelists got such a bad name that some of it rubbed off on the best ones, even Billy Sunday. These other evangelists often left a town with their bills not paid, or walked out in the middle of a revival because they thought someone had insulted them or wasn't cooperating the way they should.

For the past few years Billy had been having problems among his own staff. Naturally the newspapers reported all of these matters, and the groups who did not like Billy made especially big news out of them.

One cause for reproach was that Billy had been sued for alleged failure to live up to an agreement about payment for a book *Great Love Stories of the Bible,* written under his name by another writer.

Then Billy's private secretary, a chronic alcoholic, denounced Rodeheaver and threatened to write articles exposing the whole team. In 1912 Rody had been sued for "alleged breach of promise" and had paid $20,000.

Another staff member was in a divorce suit in 1915. That same year the whole team was sued by a Philadelphia man who had rented them his home for the campaign there. He claimed they had done more that $1500 damage to his house and its furnishings.

All these things weighed on Billy and had an effect on his work. He began to get fewer invitations to the big cities, but more to the smaller ones. His revivals were still popular in the South and Midwest, especially, but not in the East as they once had been.

Billy was not about to quit. He wanted to keep preaching, so he lowered his requirements of what had to be done before he and his team would come to a town. He still wanted a wooden tabernacle, but he decided to settle for a tent, auditorium, warehouse, or almost any other building that was big enough for the meetings.

The crowds in the smaller towns may not have been as large as in the big cities, but Billy was still busy. He led sixty-seven campaigns between 1919 and May 1930. Some of these were in middle-sized cities like Cincinnati, Dayton, Memphis, and Nashville.

Billy reduced the size of his team to only five. Now they did not need a private home to stay in, and were mostly housed in hotel rooms or homes of church members.

When Billy went into the South, he faced a problem he had not had before. Should Negroes be allowed to attend the same tabernacle services as the whites?

Back in Providence, Rhode Island, in 1918, Billy had said, "If the Negro is good enough to fight in the trenches and buy Liberty Bonds, his girl is good enough to work alongside any white girl in the munitions factories."

But when he came to a Southern town, Billy decided he should follow the local custom. This meant separate meetings for blacks and whites. When Billy tried to hold services for blacks only, the people stayed away in protest. The black leaders assured Billy they did not blame him for the situation. They blamed the local white ministers who had invited Billy without consulting black churches or making plans for them.

Despite the smaller audiences he was getting, Billy Sunday was still one of the most popular preachers in the country. In 1924 *Christian Century* magazine asked 90,000 preachers who they thought was the most influencial minister in America. More than 1000 different ministers were named in the answers that came back from all over the nation. The magazine would not tell the exact order of popularity, but Billy was in the top twenty-five. This was true respect and high praise from his fellow ministers.

During the 1920's Billy became involved in Republican party politics, and was very aware of world problems. He preached against Hitler, against Communism, and suggested that Japan and the United States might be headed for a showdown.

When Billy was asked to become a trustee of Bob Jones College in Cleveland, Tennessee, he agreed eagerly. He firmly believed that all schools must have Christian teachers, and Bob Jones was the kind of college he wanted to see grow.

The stock market crash in the fall of 1929 signaled the start of the Great Depression. It was another change of mood for America and Americans. Now many people who had been rich were poor; those who had been poor were even worse off than before. Billy saw it as a natural result of America getting away from God.

"Our great depression is not economic," Billy said. "It is spiritual, and there won't be a particle of change in the economic depression until there is a wholesale revival of the old-time religion."

It was a strong statement, but Billy Sunday was never one to hold back. The things that happened in the next few years made him even more pessimistic about whether America could ever be saved or not. A Democrat was elected president, Prohibition was repealed, Hitler came to absolute power in Germany, and our country officially recognized the new Communist Russia. All of these Billy considered bad signs. He wrote in a popular magazine, "Man cannot put the world right; our hope is in God."

Because of the times and mood of the people, other evangelists were getting out of the work. Some went into other professions, others into regular church ministries, and many began their own churches. This last was the most common choice. But Billy stayed in revivalism until the very end of his life.

The times were against Billy, though. His last full-length revival was four weeks in Mt. Holly, New Jersey, a town of just under 7,000, in 1930.

Now Billy's team was down to only himself, Nell, and Harry Clarke, the combination song leader and general helper. Billy would not give up trying to reach people for Christ, though. He kept holding revivals, even after the Mt. Holly one, but these lasted only a week or two, and were for only one church. Billy put aside his old rule of not going back to a town for a second revival, and was at many places more than once.

Many people almost forgot Billy Sunday. The big newspapers in the East did not cover his activities at all, and the newspapers in the small cities and towns where he preached were not big enough or important enough to keep Billy's name known outside their own area. Even the religious papers did not mention Billy's name very often now.

Besides losing popularity, Billy had personal and family problems on his mind.

His mother, who had lived with Billy and Nell

for 30 years after her third husband died, died herself at Winona Lake in 1918. It was the same year Billy's best friend, Dr. Chapman, died.

Death had also taken two of Billy's children. George, the oldest son, had worked on Billy's team as business manager before Nell took over. In 1923 he tried to kill himself. He was arrested for auto theft and bail jumping in 1929, and was divorced by his wife in 1930. He married again a year later, but committed suicide by jumping from a window in 1933.

William, Jr. was divorced in 1927, remarried in 1928, and was divorced again in 1929 on grounds of extreme cruelty.

Perhaps the worst sorrow for Billy was the death of his daughter Helen in 1933.

Billy was 71 years old in 1933. His health had been getting worse for several years, but he still had many invitations to preach. He was leading a revival at the First Federated Church in Des Moines, Iowa, in February. In the middle of his sermon, Billy had his first heart attack.

As the pain clutched at his chest, Billy staggered. He grabbed the pulpit to keep from falling. Harry Clarke rushed to catch him.

Billy gasped and pointed to the crowd. He was sure he was dying, but he was still thinking of the people out front first. "Don't let them go," he told Harry. "They're lost. Give them the invitation. I'd rather die on my feet seeing them come than quit."

Harry hesitated, not sure how to help his friend.

"Harry, don't let the people go without me having at least one from this meeting to go into the presence of God with," Billy whispered.

Harry signaled the choir to begin the invitation hymn. Billy held out his hand. Harry put his own hand into Billy's, but Billy thought it was someone making a decision for God.

"Thank God," Billy said.

After this first heart attack Billy took six months off to rest. He recovered, but was never in good health again. Often he had to cut short his preaching dates during the next two years, but he would not stop preaching.

The doctors had found an amazing thing about Billy Sunday. His heart was so big that it seemed to fill the whole middle of his chest. It was what was then called "athlete's heart," and was the result of the fast pace he had kept all his life.

In May, 1935, Billy had his second heart attack while preaching in Chattanooga, Tennessee. This time it was painless, and again Billy tried to keep up his preaching schedule. There were still too many people out there who were lost. He could not quit.

10

THE LAST INVITATION

IT was late October, 1935. Billy and Nell had celebrated their forty-seventh wedding anniversary the month before. Billy would be seventy-three in less than a month. His health was poor, but although he did very little preaching now, he was still getting invitations to speak. One invitation was from Aledo, Iowa, inviting Billy to speak at the thirtieth anniversary of his campaign in that town. He was also planning a two-week revival in Washington, D.C., in November.

On the weekend of October 27 an emergency came up. Billy's old friend and co-worker, Homer Rodeheaver, was preaching in the Mishawaka, Indiana, Methodist Church and was called away. He needed someone to step in for the Friday and Sunday evening services.

Rody went to see Billy at Winona Lake. As carefully as he could, Rody asked Billy if he thought he could possibly preach for him those two times.

Billy did not even have to think it over. A friend needed help, and people needed to hear about their need for Christ.

"Yes," Billy said instantly. "Yes, I sure can."

"I don't know if you should," Nell said doubtfully. "It could be too much for you."

Usually Billy listened to Nell and her ideas, but not this time. He had made up his mind. He was going to Mishawaka.

The Friday night service at the little town went well. Billy was pleased. He was tired, but he knew he was strong enough to preach again on Sunday. For his text he chose Acts 16:31: "What must I do to be saved?"

Billy preached that night as he always had, and when he gave the invitation to come forward to accept Christ, more than thirty people came. They were to be Billy Sunday's last converts for God.

On November 6, 1935, after a third heart attack, Billy Sunday died in his brother-in-law's house in Chicago. The house was across the street from one of the saloons Billy had worked so hard to close, but had seen reopened when Prohibition was repealed.

When the saloon manager heard the rumor that Billy was dead, he came across the street to the house. When he was told that Billy Sunday was indeed dead, he cried. He had been one of Billy's converts, he said, but he had slipped back into his old ways. The next day he gave up his job and disappeared.

Billy had never been afraid of death. He had never expected to live to an old age. Once in 1914, he had told a magazine editor he felt he had only ten more years of preaching in him. He had bought a cemetery plot at Forestlawn Cemetery in Chicago in 1918.

Billy had also talked to Nell about his funeral. "No sad stuff when I go," he warned her. Billy knew death was a happy time for a Christian, even though it was hard for most people to feel that way when they had lost someone they loved.

Billy's funeral was held in Moody Memorial Church in Chicago. A chilling rain fell constantly, but thousands of people ignored it and stood in line to pass by Billy's open casket. Most of them were crying.

When Billy was laid in his coffin, Nell thought his hand looked empty. It was the hand that had welcomed so many to Christ, and now it seemed too solitary to Nell. She went and got the pocket Testament Billy had always carried—even in the pocket of his nightshirt when he went to bed! She put it in his hand, and Billy Sunday was buried holding the Word of God.

Memorial services for Billy were held in other cities, too. Telegrams of sympathy came from people of all walks of life, from President Franklin D. Roosevelt and John D. Rockefeller, Jr. to the leaders of the baseball world, and from many men and women Billy had converted and led to a changed life.

On Billy's tombstone was carved the verse from 2 Timothy 4:7: "I have fought the good fight; I have finished my course; I have kept the faith."

It was hard to believe that the vital, energetic, active Billy Sunday was dead. He had led more than three-hundred separate revivals all over the country and had spoken to more than 100 million people. (Remember that this was before the days of TV, and most of his meetings were before radio or even loudspeakers were available.) He had welcomed more than one million who came down the "sawdust trail" to Jesus.

Billy Sunday, who once said, "I'd stand on my head in a mud puddle if I thought it would help me win souls to Christ," was finally resting from his labors.